RHODE ISLAND PATRIOTS

Their Lives, Contributions, and Burial Sites

JOE FARRELL • LAWRENCE KNORR • JOE FARLEY

SUNBURY
PRESS

Mechanicsburg, PA USA

Published by Sunbury Press, Inc.
Mechanicsburg, Pennsylvania

SUNBURY
P R E S S®
www.sunburypress.com

For information about special discounts for bulk purchases, please contact Sunbury Press Orders Dept. at (855) 338-8359 or orders@sunburypress.com.

To request one of our authors for speaking engagements or book signings, please contact Sunbury Press Publicity Dept. at publicity@sunburypress.com.

FIRST SUNBURY PRESS EDITION: February 2025

Set in Adobe Garamond | Interior design by Crystal Devine | Cover by Lawrence Knorr | Edited by the authors.

Publisher's Cataloging-in-Publication Data
Names: Farrell, Joe, author | Farley, Joe, author | Knorr, Lawrence, author.
Title: Rhode Island patriots : their lives, contributions, and burial sites / Joe Farrell Lawrence Knorr Joe Farley.
Description: First trade paperback edition. | Mechanicsburg, PA : Sunbury Press, 2025.
Summary: The individuals from Rhode Island who played prominent roles in the founding of the USA are detailed.
Identifiers: ISBN 979-8-88819-298-6 (softcover).
Subjects: HISTORY / United States / Revolutionary Period (1775-1800) | BIOGRAPHY & AUTOBIOGRAPHY / Political.

Designed in the USA
0 1 1 2 3 5 8 13 21 34 55

For the Love of Books!

Contents

Contents

Introduction

The little Ocean State was the first to call for a Continental Congress in 1774 and the first to renounce British rule on May 4, 1776, two months before the Declaration of Independence. Though Rhode Island was an early signer of the Articles of Confederation, they resisted signing the new US Constitution to the last becoming our thirteenth state of the thirteen original colonies. Perhaps the biggest event in the colony was the Battle of Rhode Island, which was at the end of a three-year British occupation of Newport.

The top Rhode Islander involved in the American Revolution was actually buried in Savannah, Georgia. Nathanael Greene was a Quaker who took up arms and rose to the highest levels in the Continental Army, as George Washington's second or third in command at different points in the War. Greene led the successful Southern Campaign that helped turn the tide.

Of course, the contributions of Stephen Hopkins are numerous. He was a governor of the colony and a signer of the Continental Association and the Declaration of Independence. Unfortunately, he was likely suffering from Parkinson's Disease, which became more pronounced in his later years. His rivalry with Samuel Ward was bitter, but the two mended the fence in the Continental Congress.

Samuel Ward, the son of a governor, became governor himself, trading the seat with Stephen Hopkins. The two then attended the Continental Congress where Ward was one of the first Congressmen from Rhode Island. He died in Philadelphia from smallpox after signing the Continental Association, and before signing the Declaration of Independence. His remains were returned to Rhode Island.

John Collins was another governor of Rhode Island. He also signed the Articles of Confederation, which made him eligible for this book. He was also a close friend of Benjamin Franklin.

After Samuel Ward's death, William Ellery was appointed to the Continental Congress, where he signed the Declaration of Independence and the Articles of Confederation. He was also an early abolitionist.

Henry Marchant, prior to the Revolution, traveled to Scotland with Benjamin Franklin and participated in many of the meetings with David Hume. Marchant was later a Continental Congressman.

Though the smallest colony in size, Rhode Island's contributions certainly exceeded expectations.

Nathanael Greene
(1742–1786)

Liberator of the South

Buried at Johnson Square,
Savannah, Georgia.

————•◦•————

Military

Nathanael Greene, a native of Rhode Island, was a major general during the American Revolution. He was one of three men, besides George Washington and Henry Knox, to serve the entire duration of the war. Greene was second in command to only Washington, and towards the end of the war turned the tide in the British-ravaged south.

————◦•◦————

Nathanael Greene was born on "Forge Farm" in Potowomut, Rhode Island, on August 7, 1742. He was the son of Nathanael Greene (1707-1768), a Quaker farmer and smith. He was descended from John Greene Sr. and Samuel Gorton who were both early settlers of Warwick, Rhode Island. His mother was Mary Mott, the second wife of Nathanael senior. Greene was mostly self-educated and influenced by Reverend Ezra Stiles, who was later a president of Yale University.

Around the time of his father's death, Greene moved to Coventry, Rhode Island and took charge of the family's foundry. There he also established a public school and was chosen to the Rhode Island Assembly, to which he was re-elected several times. He married Catharine Littlefield in July 1774 with whom he had six children who survived infancy.

Though a Quaker, he eschewed that faith's commitment to pacifism in the face of American independence. In August 1774, Greene helped

Original portrait of Nathanael Greene painted from life in
1783 by Charles Willson Peale.

organize a local militia and began reading extensively about military tac-
tics. In December, he was on a committee to revise militia laws. This
focus on the military led to his expulsion from the Quakers.

On May 8, 1775, Greene was promoted to major general of the
Rhode Island Army of Observation that formed in response to the siege
of Boston. The Continental Congress appointed him a brigadier general
in the Continental Army the following month. Washington assigned
Greene to command the city of Boston after it was evacuated by the
British in March 1776.

On August 9, 1776, Greene was promoted to major general and was
given command of the Continental Army on Long Island. He led the
construction of entrenchments and fortifications but was prevented by
illness from taking part in the Battle of Long Island. Greene advocated
for a retreat from New York City and was then stationed on the New

Equestrian statue of Nathanael Greene at Guilford Court House Battlefield (photo by Lawrence Knorr).

Jersey side of the Hudson. After the Americans retreated, Greene commanded one of the two columns at the Battle of Trenton. He urged to press immediately on to Princeton but was rebuffed by his peers.

During the Philadelphia campaign, at the Battle of Brandywine, Greene commanded the reserves. At Germantown, his troops distinguished themselves but were late to the field. In March of 1778, Washington appointed him Quartermaster General at Valley Forge with the understanding he would retain command of troops in the field. Greene was in command of the right wing at Monmouth in late June of 1778.

In August of 1778, Greene returned to his home state of Rhode Island with Lafayette to command the land forces in cooperation with French Admiral d'Estaing at the successful Battle of Rhode Island. Back in New Jersey in June of 1780, Greene was in command at the Battle of Springfield, putting an end to British ambitions in the north. In August, he resigned as Quartermaster General after a long dispute with Congress regarding how the army should be administered and supplied. Washington appointed Greene commander at West Point where he presided over the condemnation of Major John André on September 29, 1780.

On October 5, 1780, Washington appointed Greene as commander of the southern theater, giving him charge of all troops from Delaware to Georgia. He took command at Hillsborough, North Carolina, on December 3, 1780, replacing Horatio Gates. Greene decided to divide his troops in the face of a superior force under Cornwallis. At Kings Mountain in 1780, Colonel William Campbell captured or killed the entire British force. At Cowpens, on January 17, 1781, General Daniel Morgan captured or killed 90% of the British forces. With over 800 prisoners in tow, the Americans began a strategic retreat to draw Cornwallis out, leveraging light cavalry to harass the enemy. The force successfully crossed the Dan River ahead of the British and reached safety in Virginia. Some have referred to this one of the most masterful military achievements of all time.

Now strengthened by reinforcements, Greene's army re-crossed the Dan River and faced Cornwallis at the Battle of Guilford Court House on ground chosen by Greene. As the Americans were turning the British flank, Cornwallis ordered the cannons to fire on his own troops and the Americans. This repulsed the attack, though Cornwallis lost as many of his own as his enemy. Greene then ordered a tactical retreat that further battered and exhausted Cornwallis. The British withdrew towards Wilmington, North Carolina, while Greene now turned towards the liberation of the low country of South Carolina, achieved by June 1781. After the Battle of Eutaw Springs, the British were now forced to the coast where Greene eventually pinned them at Charleston until the end of the war.

Regarding the Southern Campaign, though defeated in every pitched battle by a superior enemy, Greene managed to divide, elude, and tire his opponent through long marches. The Americans chipped away at a British force that was not being reinforced. Others in the campaign were Polish engineer Tadeusz Kościuszko, cavalry officers Henry ("Light-Horse Harry") Lee and William Washington, and partisan leaders Thomas Sumter, Andrew Pickens, Elijah Clarke, and Francis Marion. In the end, Greene had liberated the southern states from British control. When the Treaty of Paris ended the war, British forces controlled a couple of southern coastal cities, but Greene controlled the rest.

After the war, Greene was an original member of the Rhode Island Society of the Cincinnati, serving as president until his death. Several of the southern states granted him lands and money. He sold most of the land to pay war debts associated with his role as Quartermaster General. He kept the "Mulberry Grove" plantation granted to him near Savannah, Georgia.

Grave of Nathanael Greene beneath Johnson Square in Savannah, Georgia (photo by Joe Farrell).

He was offered the post of Secretary of War by President Washington but declined.

Greene died at "Mulberry Grove" on June 19, 1786, at the age of only 43. He was initially interred at the Graham Vault in Colonial Park Cemetery in Savannah. On October 14, 1902, his remains were moved to a monument in Johnson Square in Savannah.

There are many memorials to Nathanael Greene:

- There are many cities, counties, and parks named after him across the country.
- Ships: four Coast Guard cutters, a James Madison-class nuclear submarine, an Army cargo ship, a Liberty class steam merchant, and a 128-foot Army tug which is still in service today.

■ A large portrait hangs in the Rhode Island State House, and a statue stands outside the building.

■ A cenotaph to him stands in the Old Forge Burial Ground in Warwick.

■ His statue, with that of Roger Williams, represents the state of Rhode Island in the National Hall of Statuary in the Capitol.

■ In Washington, there is a bronze equestrian statue by Henry Kirke Brown at the center of Stanton Park.

Detail from Nathanael Greene's monument (photo by Joe Farrell).

■ A small statue by Lewis Iselin, Jr. is outside the Philadelphia Museum of Art.

■ An equestrian statue designed by Francis H. Packer at the site of the Battle of Guilford Courthouse.

■ A statue stands in the middle of the traffic circle between Greene Street and McGee Street in downtown Greensboro.

■ Greeneville, Tennessee and Greene County, Tennessee are named after him.

■ The city of Greenville, South Carolina, also named for him, unveiled a statue designed by T. J. Dixon and James Nelson at the corner of South Main and Broad Streets.

■ A bronze statue of Greene by sculptor Chas Fagan is in St. Clair Park, in Greensburg, Pennsylvania.

■ A statue is in Valley Forge National Military Park, Pennsylvania.

■ The Nathanael Greene Homestead is in Coventry, Rhode Island.

John Collins
(1717 – 1795)

Rhode Island Representative

Buried at Collins Burial Ground,
Newport, Rhode Island.

Articles of Confederation

John Collins was the third governor of Rhode Island, a Continental Congressman, and a signer of the Articles of Confederation. He is credited with casting the deciding vote in Rhode Island to adopt the U.S. Constitution.

John Collins was born in Newport, Rhode Island, on June 8, 1717, the son of Samuel and Elizabeth Collins. He was a businessman and merchant by trade, selling merchandise in Newport that he had acquired through trade as far away as the Mississippi River. He married Mary Avery, the daughter of John Avery of Boston, and the couple had a son also named John Collins and a daughter Abigail.

During the War of Independence, Collins was sent by Rhode Island to the Continental Congress where he served from 1778 to 1780 and again from 1782 to 1783. Collins was involved in activities regarding the army, navy, and finance.

After the war, Collins was elected Governor of Rhode Island, serving from 1786 to 1790. An article in *The Universal Asylum* magazine from June 1790 related the closeness of Collins and Benjamin Franklin. The article stated:

John Collins was one of Franklin's most intimate acquaintance. This was a boy who was very fond of reading. With him, Franklin often disputed on various subjects. Like most young disputants, they were very warm and very desirous of consulting each other. One subject was started, which produced a longer discussion than usual. It was respecting the propriety of educating the female sex, and their abilities for acquiring knowledge. Collins endeavored to show, that they were naturally unequal to the talk of study and that a learned education was improper for them. Franklin supported the opposite opinion, with much warmth, though he was occasionally staggered, more by the greater fluency of his adversary, than by the strength of his arguments.

After the U.S. Constitution was drafted in Philadelphia in 1787, it was sent to the 13 states to be ratified. Each state had to decide whether or not to hold a state convention and then proceed to vote. Rhode Island lagged the other colonies in approving the Constitution, holding out for

There is no known portrait of John Collins. This image is of the historic Colony House in Newport, Rhode Island, which was the seat of government in colonial times.

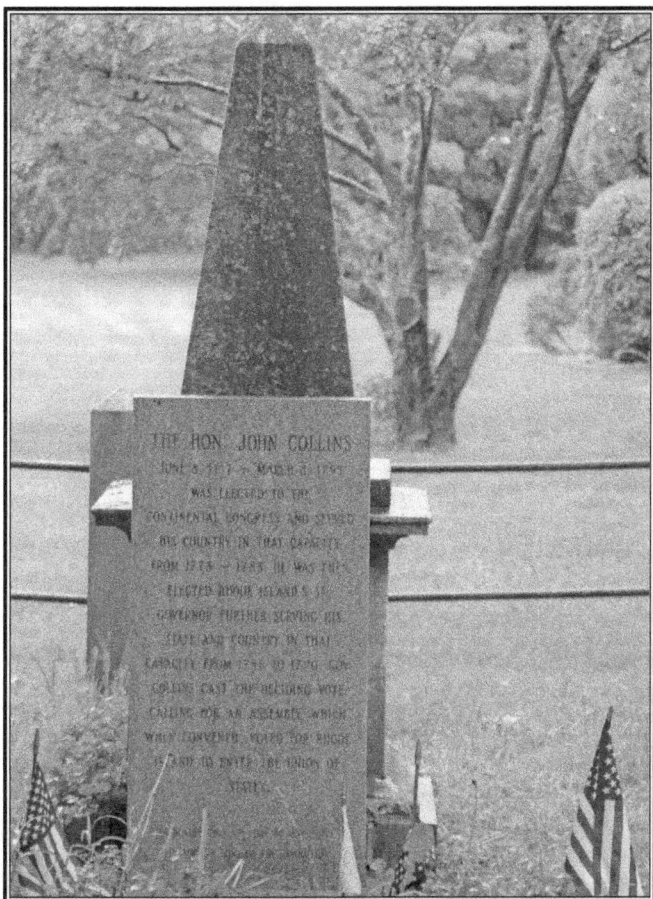

The grave of John Collins at the Collins Burial Ground, Newport, Rhode Island (photo by Lawrence Knorr).

a Bill of Rights. During this time, Rhode Island was in effect an independent nation with Collins as its head of state. The state remained deeply divided even after the Bill of Rights was introduced, but Collins called for a vote for a convention anyway. In the end, he was the one to cast the deciding vote that called for a state convention in Rhode Island. Without his vote, Rhode Island would not have adopted the Constitution.

Following the ratification of the Constitution, Collins was nominated for a seat in the First Congress, but he refused it even though he was elected. Collins wife, Mary, had died in 1788 at the age of 53. Collins also left the governorship in 1790.

John Collins died in Newport on March 4, 1795, at the age of 78. He was laid to rest in the Collins family burial ground on their Newport, Rhode Island estate, "Brenton Neck." By 1854, the burial ground had become so rundown that relatives restored the graves and stones. In 2002, the Sons of the American Revolution placed a stone next to his cenotaph that reads, "The Hon. John Collins, June 8, 1717-March 8, 1795, was elected to the Continental Congress and Served His Country in that Capacity from 1778-1783. He was Then Elected Rhode Island's 3rd Governor, Further Serving His State and Country in that Capacity from 1786 to 1790. Gov. Collins Cast the Deciding Vote Calling for an Assembly, Which When Convened Voted for Rhode Island to Enter the Union of States."

Abigail Collins, the daughter of John and Mary, married John Warren, a surgeon in the Continental Army and founder of Harvard Medical School. Warren was the younger brother of Dr. Joseph Warren. Collins' grandson, John Collins Covell (1823-1887) was a principal of the Virginia and West Virginia schools for the deaf and blind. Collins' great-great-grandson, Collins Lawton Balch (1834-1910) was a successful businessman and merchant in Rhode Island.

The Rhode Island Society of the Sons of the American Revolution holds an annual observance of Rhode Island Independence Day every May 4th at Collins' grave.

William Ellery
(1727 – 1820)

Early Abolitionist

Buried at Common Burying Ground,
Newport, Rhode Island.

———•◦•———

Declaration of Independence • Articles of Confederation

This Founder once wrote a letter to one of his grandsons enumerating the jobs he had been employed in over the years. Putting pen to paper he stated, "I have been a clerk of the court, a quack lawyer, a member of Congress, one of the Lords of the Admiralty, a judge, a loan officer, and finally a collector of the customs, and thus, not without many difficulties, but as honestly, thank God, as most men, I have got through the journey of a varied and sometimes anxious life." As part of that journey, he added his signature to the document declaring American independence. His name was William Ellery.

———•◦•———

Ellery was born on December 22, 1727, in Newport, Rhode Island. His father was a graduate of Harvard and a wealthy merchant. He was initially educated by his father and eventually also found his way to Harvard from which he graduated at the age of twenty. He then returned to Newport where he first attempted to follow in his father's shoes as a merchant.

Ellery married twice, first in 1750 to Ann Remington who died in 1764 and again in 1767 when he wed Abigail Cary. In the course of these

Portrait of William Ellery, artist unknown.

marriages, he fathered at least sixteen children, though some put the number at nineteen. Only one other signer, Carter Braxton, is recorded as fathering more. Needless to say, providing for a family of this size took a lot of his energy, though clearly not all of it.

Ellery, as stated in his aforementioned letter, worked a number of jobs until at age forty he achieved a life's ambition and began to practice law. He was a successful lawyer working in both his home state and nearby Massachusetts. At this same time, he became involved in the political scene becoming active in the Sons of Liberty. Like many of the patriots of his day he strongly opposed the Stamp Act and the Intolerable Acts.

In 1776, Samuel Ward, a former Rhode Island governor who was one of the two Rhode Island representatives to the Continental Congress, died after contracting smallpox. Ellery was the choice to replace him. Thus he arrived in Congress shortly before the Declaration of Independence was adopted and signed. In both the play and the movie *1776* it is the other

Marker honoring William Ellery.

Rhode Island delegate, Stephen Hopkins, who is portrayed as finding a spot where he could see each man's face as he signed the Declaration. In reality, it was Ellery who did so. Describing the scene he said, "I was determined to see how they all looked as they signed what might be their death warrant. I placed myself beside the secretary Charles Thomson and eyed each closely as he affixed his name to the document. Undaunted resolution was displayed on every countenance."

During the Revolution, the British seized Newport and burned Ellery's home to the ground. During the occupation, he and his family fled to Dighton, Massachusetts where they resided until it was safe to return to their home and begin the rebuilding process.

After joining Congress, Ellery would remain a member of that body for eight of the next ten years. In 1922, the *Altoona Tribune* described him as one of its most influential members. During this period, he also signed the Articles of Confederation and served on numerous committees including war wounded, army purchases, and public accounts.

In 1786, Ellery left Congress and returned to Rhode Island to attend to his personal affairs, most notably shoring up his financial situation. He worked a number of jobs until 1790 when President Washington appointed him customs collector for Newport. The appointment solidified him financially and he held the post until his death.

Ellery was one of three signers of the Declaration of Independence who lived into their nineties, dying at the age of 92 on February 15, 1820. He was laid to rest in the Common Burying Ground in Newport, Rhode Island.

There is an annual commemoration held at his grave every July 4th sponsored by the Sons of the Revolution and the William Ellery Chapter of the Daughters of the American Revolution. A town in New York and an avenue in Middletown, Rhode Island are named in his honor.

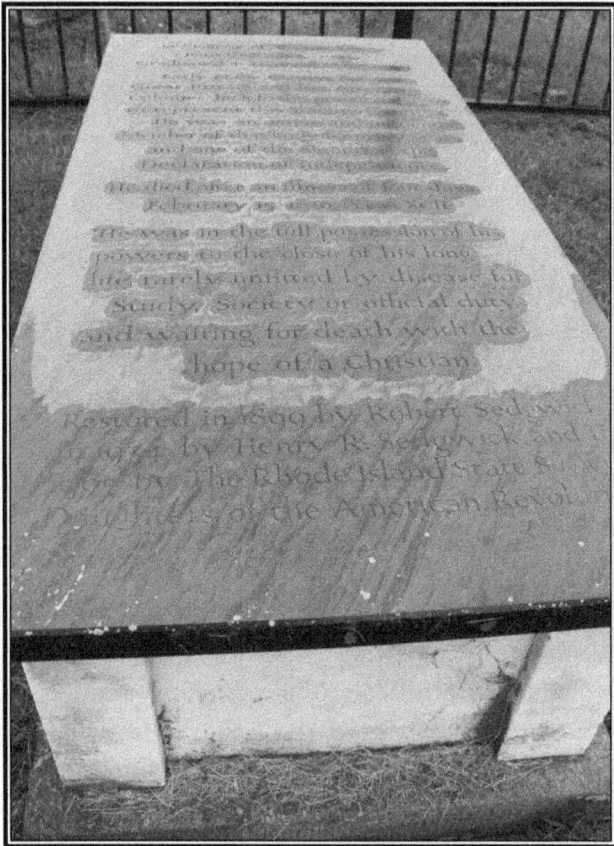

The grave of William Ellery at Common Burying Ground & Island Cemetery in Newport, Rhode Island (photo by Lawrence Knorr).

Stephen Hopkins
(1707–1785)

"Greatest Statesman of Rhode Island"

Buried at North Burial Ground
Providence, Rhode Island

**Continental Congress • Continental Association
Declaration of Independence**

Stephen Hopkins was a Quaker colonial governor of Rhode Island and Providence Plantations who sided with the Patriots and signed the Continental Association and Declaration of Independence as a member of the Continental Congress. In John Trumbull's famous painting, *The Declaration of Independence*, Hopkins is seen standing in the back with his distinctive hat. Hopkins was also a judge, educator, merchant ship owner, and surveyor.

Hopkins was born March 7, 1707, in Cranston, Rhode Island. He was the first son and second of nine children of the itinerant farmer William Hopkins and his wife, Ruth (née Wilkinson) Hopkins. The elder Hopkins was the son of William Hopkins, a prominent Rhode Island politician, and the grandson of Thomas Hopkins, one of the original settlers of the Providence Plantations, sailing from England with his cousin, Benedict Arnold, in 1635. Arnold was the first governor of Rhode Island following its charter in 1663 and was an ancestor to the famous general and traitor of the American Revolution. The family tradition, in some genealogies, linking Hopkins to Stephen Hopkins of the *Mayflower* is unfounded.

Stephen Hopkins

Hopkins' mother was the granddaughter of Lieutenant Lawrence Wilkinson of Charles I's army, who was taken prisoner by the Scots at the surrender of Newcastle-on-Tyne on October 22, 1644. He lost his lands and thus emigrated to New England circa 1646 as an indentured servant and was in Providence by 1652. He was a freeman by 1658 and became a deputy of the General Court, a soldier in the Indian wars, and a member of the Colonial Assembly in 1659.

Hopkins grew up on a modest farm in Scituate, Rhode Island. His mother started his education by teaching him to read and write. His uncle and grandfather taught him mathematics and surveying, and he read the English classics in his grandfather's library. He learned farming from his father, who gave him his first farmland at 19.

Also at age 19, on October 9, 1726, Hopkins married Sarah Scott, a relation of Anne Hutchinson and Joseph Jenks, with whom he had seven children before she developed a debilitating illness in the 1750s. She committed suicide at age 47 in 1753. Hopkins married Ann Smith, a widow, in 1755.

At age 23 in 1730, Hopkins began his public career as a justice of the peace in Scituate, Rhode Island. In 1732, he was elected the town clerk, a post he held until 1741, and to a seat in the General Assembly, where he served until 1752, for his first tenure. He was Speaker of the Assembly from 1738 to 1744 and in 1749. Despite not having a law degree, Hopkins was named Chief Justice of the Court of Common Pleas for Rhode Island, and in 1747, was appointed as a Justice on the Rhode Island Supreme Court, serving until May 1749. From May 1751 to May 1755, Hopkins became the Chief Justice of this court. During these years, he became President of the Scituate Town Council.

Hopkins sold his farm in Scituate in 1742 and moved to Providence. Here, he became a merchant and outfitted ships with his brother, Esek Hopkins. They traded in wool and cloth. He was part owner, with Sheriff John Mawney and his son, Colonel Peter Mawney, of the privateering vessel *Reprisal* in 1745. The painter John Greenwood included Hopkins (drunk and dozing at the table) in his satirical 1750s painting *Sea Captains Carousing in Surinam*. Later, Hopkins became involved in manufacturing and was partners with brothers Moses and John Brown in establishing the Hope Furnace. They made pig iron, which was used in the Revolutionary War. Son Rufus Hopkins managed the foundry for four decades.

Following the death of his first wife, Hopkins became more interested in colonial politics, supporting the colonies in developing their own voice in matters affecting them. He helped establish a public subscription library and was the first chancellor of Rhode Island College, which became Brown University. He became a member of the American Philosophical Society of Newport.

In 1754, he served as a delegate to the Colonial Congress meeting in Albany, New York, with 150 members of the Iroquois Nations. The meeting aimed to prevent the natives from joining with the French and to create an alliance with the colonies that granted them additional rights. Unfortunately, the colonies did not approve the agreement, but it was a precursor to later attempts at unified action. Hopkins penned a history of the proceedings in *A True Representation of the Plan formed at Albany, in 1754, for Uniting all the British Northern Colonies*. He also met Ben Franklin in Albany, and the two remained friends for the rest of their lives.

In 1755, Hopkins was elected Governor of Rhode Island, serving for nine of the next fifteen years. During this time, he became embroiled in political intrigue with rival governor Samuel Ward, who served when Hopkins was not. The two engaged in what became known as the Ward-Hopkins War or Ward-Hopkins Controversy between Hopkins' "Providence faction" and Ward's "Newport faction." In 1757, Ward accused Hopkins of using his office for personal gain. Enraged, Hopkins brought countercharges, resulting in a court case that had to be held in Massachusetts due to the fractious nature of Rhode Island. James Otis represented Hopkins, and the two became friends, but Otis lost this case, and Hopkins had to pay all the court costs. Hopkins bitterly threatened to "blow Ward's brains out" and subsequently lost the next election to William Greene, a leader of the Ward Faction. However, when Ward died suddenly in 1758, the General Assembly selected Hopkins as his successor, bypassing Ward.

Hopkins started two very successful newspapers, the *Providence Gazette* and *Country Journal*, in 1762. He used them to his political advantage, especially concerning the Stamp Act and the controversy regarding currency; Ward supported hard currency, and Hopkins supported paper, and the two continued to tangle. Hopkins, meanwhile, was the only colonial governor not to take an oath in support of the Stamp Act. In 1766, he penned a pamphlet, *The Grievances of the American Colonies*, calling for the basic human rights of the colonists. Ten years before the Declaration of Independence, Hopkins wrote:

> Liberty is the greatest blessing that men enjoy, and slavery is the greatest curse that human nature is capable of. Hence it is a matter of the utmost importance to men, which of the two shall be their Portion. Absolute liberty is perhaps incompatible with any kind of government. The safety resulting from society and the advantage of just and equal laws hath caused men to forego some part of

their natural liberty and submit to government. This appears to be the most rational account of its beginning; although it must be confessed, mankind has by no means agreed about it: some have found its original in the divine appointment; others have thought it took its rise from power . . .

Finally, in 1768, the two rivals agreed not to run against each other, and Josias Lyndon was elected governor as a compromise candidate.

In 1769, Hopkins coordinated the construction of a telescope in Providence and personally took measurements of Venus's transit across the Sun in 1769.

In 1770, Hopkins returned as the Chief Justice of the Supreme Court of Rhode Island. This put him in the middle of the *Gaspée* Affair beginning in June 1772. The HMS *Gaspée*, led by Lieutenant William Duddingston, was a customs enforcement vessel sent by the British to monitor the Navigation Acts long set by the British Parliament to control trade in the colonies. Captain Abraham Whipple, sailing a vessel owned by Hopkins' business associates, John and Moses Brown, did not appreciate the incursion in Narragansett Bay on the colonies' sovereignty and lured the British vessel into a chase. The British captain did not immediately realize the ruse and soon ran aground on a shallow point near Warwick, Rhode Island, now known as Gaspée Point. The Sons of Liberty, led by John Brown, alerted to the opportunity, sailed out to the customs ship, arrested the crew, and set it afire, burning it to the waterline on the night of June 9 to 10. Lieutenant Duddingston was wounded in the raid, and he and his men were taken ashore as booty.

Throughout the colonies, fellow Patriots saw this as a heroic effort. The Rhode Island court issued arrest warrants for Duddingston and his crew for attempting to seize goods in violation of Rhode Island law. Meanwhile, the British in London were outraged and sent orders to the Supreme Court in Rhode Island to prosecute the perpetrators. Chief Justice Stephen Hopkins refused to sign any court orders sent by the British. Using his influence, he told the commissioners sent from London who investigated the incident that, though he shared their outrage, none of the men could be identified and "neither apprehend by my own order nor suffer any executive officer in the colony to do it, for the purpose of transportation to England for trial." Realizing the effort would be fruitless, the British gave up, never charging anyone. Unknown to them, one of Hopkins' relatives was among the raiders and Hopkins, his subordinates, and others coordinated to lose evidence, threaten witnesses, and discredit those who testified. Meanwhile, the British inquiry spurred the creation of Committees of Correspondence in the colonies.

Hopkins, who owned six slaves, including a man, a woman, and three boys, freed the man, named Saint Jago, on October 28, 1772. He wrote on the manumission document:

> But, principally, and most of all, finding that the merciful and beneficent goodness of Almighty God; by the blessed Gospel of Jesus Christ our Lord: hath by the blessed Spirit taught all, who honestly obey its Divine Dictates, that, the keeping any of his rational Creatures in Bondage, who are capable of taking care of, and providing for themselves in a State of Freedom: is, altogether inconsistent with his Holy and Righteous Will.

However, he did not free the woman, Fibbo, even though it cost him membership in the Quaker meeting. He felt she and her children required care and could not live independently. Early in 1774, at a meeting of the General Assembly of Rhode Island, Hopkins introduced a bill prohibiting the importation of slaves. It was one of the first anti-slave trade laws in the colonies.

He and his former enemy, Samuel Ward, were sent as delegates to the First Continental Congress. There, he declared: ". . . powder and ball will decide this question. The gun and bayonet alone will finish the contest in which we are engaged, and any of you who cannot bring your minds to this mode of adjusting this question had better retire in time." He and Ward both signed the Continental Association on October 20, 1774.

Speaking of the 100th anniversary of this First Congress, orator Henry Armitt Brown described Hopkins, who had developed palsy in his old age:

. . . yonder sits the oldest of them all. His form is bent, his thin locks, fringing a forehead bowed with age and honorable service, and his hands shake tremulously as he folds them in his lap. It is Stephen Hopkins.

John Adams wrote in his diary at that time about Hopkins:

Mr. [Francis Lightfoot] Lee [of Virginia], Mr. [Christopher] Gadsden [of South Carolina], were sensible men, and very cheerful, but Governor Hopkins of Rhode Island, above seventy years of age, kept us all alive. Upon business, his experience and judgment were very useful. But when the business of the evening was over, he kept us in conversation till eleven, and sometimes twelve o'clock. His custom was to drink nothing all day, nor till eight o'clock in the evening, and then his beverage was Jamaica spirit and water. It gave him wit, humor, anecdotes, science and learning. He had read Greek, Roman, and British history, and was familiar with English poetry, particularly Pope, Thomson, and Milton, and the flow of his soul made all his reading our own, and seemed to bring to recollection in all of us, all we had ever read . . . Hopkins never drank to excess, but all he drank was immediately not only converted into wit, sense, knowledge, and good humor, but inspired us with similar qualities.

After the Battles of Lexington and Concord in April 1775, the Second Continental Congress convened. Hopkins signed the Olive Branch Petition that summer. In February 1776, he arranged for his younger brother, Esek, to be named the first commander-in-chief of the Continental Navy. On March 26, 1776, while in Philadelphia, Samuel Ward died suddenly, leaving a vacancy in the Second Continental Congress. He was replaced by William Ellery.

Rhode Island declared independence from Great Britain on May 4, 1776. Hopkins and Ellery, at the Congress, knew this and participated in the debates. At one point on July 1, a thunderstorm gathered outside the hall while John Dickinson rambled into his second hour of speaking.

Suddenly, there was a thunderclap, and Hopkins dropped the cane on which his head had been perched, snapping it up quickly.

John Penn of North Carolina, believing the man was frightened, whispered to Hopkins reassuringly, "There is a rod atop the State House—one of Dr. Franklin's inventions—the celebrated lightning rod. If by chance a bolt of lightning should strike the belfry, that same rod would run the bolt into the ground."

Hopkins turned to Penn and roared, "I don't give a damn about any rod or lightning bolt. I'm just tired of Dickinson's long-winded harangue!"

Ellery and Hopkins signed the Declaration of Independence. Hopkins was the second oldest to sign, only one year younger than Ben Franklin, who was 70. Though his body shook from palsy, making it difficult to walk, Hopkins held his shaking right hand with his left as he signed, saying, "My hand trembles, but my heart does not." Thus ended his stint in Congress.

For the next three years, Hopkins occasionally participated in the Rhode Island Council of War and at conventions of the New England States, serving as president of the 1777 convention. He was elected to participate in the discussions about the Articles of Confederation but soon returned to Rhode Island due to his health. Hopkins died in Providence, Rhode Island, on July 13, 1785, at age 78. He was interred in the North Burial Ground, accompanied by a large, distinguished funeral procession. One side of his obelisk reads:

> Sacred to the Memory of the Illustrious Stephen Hopkins. Of Revolutionary Fame. Attested by his Signature to the Declaration of Our National Independence. Great in Council, From Sagacity of Mind: Magnanimous in Sentiment: Firm in Purpose: and Good, As Great, from Benevolent Heart.

Hopkins is remembered in many ways. Hopkinton, Rhode Island, was named after him. The SS *Stephen Hopkins* was a liberty ship that was the first US ship to sink a German surface vessel in World War II. His home, originally at the corner of Hopkins and South Main Streets in

Providence, was moved twice to different locations on Hopkins Street, now at number 15, on the edge of the Brown University campus.

Many have written well of Hopkins over the years. In his diary, Reverend Ezra Stiles called him ". . . a man of penetrating astucious Genius, full of Subtlety, deep Cunning, intriguing & enterprising . . . a man of a Noble fortitude & resolution" and "a glorious Patriot!"

The historian Irving Berdine Richman dubbed Hopkins "the greatest statesman of Rhode Island."

Grave of Stephen Hopkins

Henry Marchant
(1741–1796)

Liberty Lawyer

Buried at Common Burial Ground,
Newport, Rhode Island.

Articles of Confederation

Henry Marchant was an attorney from Newport, Rhode Island, who served as the attorney general of that state and a member of the state legislature. As a delegate to the Continental Congress, he signed the Articles of Confederation. He supported the U.S. Constitution and was appointed the first federal judge for the U.S. District Court of Rhode Island.

Henry Marchant was born on April 9, 1741, in Edgartown, on the island of Martha's Vineyard, in Massachusetts, the son of Huxford Marchant, a sea captain, and his wife, Sarah (née Butler) Marchant. The Marchant family descended from John Marchant, born in 1571, in Yeovil, Somerset, England. Sarah Marchant died in 1745 when Henry was a toddler. His father then married Isabel Ward, the daughter and sister of the governors of Rhode Island, Richard Ward and Samuel Ward. When Huxford Marchant died while in Liberia or the West Indies in July 1747, stepmother Isabel remained to raise her young stepson in a world of wealth and privilege.

When Henry was of school age, Isabel sent him to a prestigious academy in Newport. He then went to Philadelphia College (now the

University of Pennsylvania), where he was introduced to Benjamin Franklin. Marchant graduated in 1762. Next, he studied law in the offices of Judge Edmund Trowbridge of Cambridge, Massachusetts.

Following his legal training, Marchant was admitted to the Rhode Island bar and opened a practice in Newport. He was the only "liberty lawyer" in the colony but was well-connected with local officials and the church. Marchant was the personal attorney for his uncle Samuel Ward.

On January 8, 1765, Marchant married Rebecca Cooke at Trinity Church in Newport. The couple had four children between 1766 and 1771: Sarah, Henry, William, and Elizabeth. Only Sarah and Elizabeth lived to adulthood.

Marchant then got involved in local politics. On December 4, 1767, he was elected to the Council of Newport. About three years later, Marchant was elected the attorney general for the colony, serving from October 1770 to May 1777.

Marchant was a bright young man, curious about science, and mathematically inclined. In 1769, he assisted Dr. Ezra Stiles, a well-known intellectual, Congregationalist pastor, and founder of Brown University, in observing and plotting the transit of Venus. Stiles was a member of the American Philosophical Society in Philadelphia and later became the president of Yale University.

In 1771, Marchant was named an agent for Rhode Island in England, and he visited the mother country for eleven months seeking recompense for the colony for a couple of court cases. He had quite a send-off, as recounted by David Lovejoy in the *William and Mary Quarterly*:

> Henry Marchant's departure for England on July 8, 1771, was a significant occasion in the social life of Newport. Nearly a score of friends, reluctant to see him leave, accompanied him in chaises and on horseback as far as Bristol Ferry, eight miles northward on the way to Providence and Boston. His well-wishers included his wife, of course, and his "honord Mother in Law," but also Joseph Clarke, General Treasurer of the colony; William Ellery, later member of the Continental Congress; Josias Lyndon, former Governor; and the Reverend Ezra Stiles, Marchant's minister. (Stiles had good

reason to be pleasant since Marchant had tucked three guineas "gratuity" into his pocket before they left Newport.) At Bristol Ferry, there was "heavy parting from such good Friends"; several crossed over to the mainland with him and after a "Repetition of parting Feelings," dropped by the wayside at the homes of relatives. Richard Olney accompanied young Marchant to Providence; Mrs. Marchant prolonged her leave-taking and stayed with her husband all the way to Boston, where he was to embark.

Marchant kept a descriptive journal of his thoughts and encounters while in London. He conducted business before the Privy Council in London and traveled through Scotland with Ben Franklin, traveling in the highest intellectual and political circles. In Scotland, the two dined together often and met with David Hume. They toured the universities in Edinburgh and Glasgow. Marchant also participated in the sixty-sixth birthday party for Franklin. Back in London, Marchant was introduced to the historian Catharine Macaulay, and the two had numerous dinners together, discussing English history and the politics of the time. He maintained correspondence with Macauley, who was a radical thinker. Macauley later visited the United States, calling on Richard Henry Lee, George Washington, and others.

With the burning of the *Gaspee* off Rhode Island in June 1772, Marchant's business became more difficult. He bade farewell to Franklin, who was "ill of the Gout in one Foot," and headed home in late July 1772. The voyage turned out to be difficult when, in mid-ocean, a fire consumed the ship's galley thanks to a pot of boiling pitch left unattended. Fortunately, the fire did not reach the thirty barrels of gunpowder in the hold, and Marchant was safely back in Boston on September 20.

By May 1773, Marchant was active in the heated political discussions of the time, fresh off his experiences in England. As tensions mounted with Great Britain, Marchant was a member of Rhode Island's Sons of Liberty and Committee of Correspondence. A son, William, was born in 1774.

When Marchant's term as attorney general concluded, the Rhode Island General Assembly appointed him to the Continental Congress on

May 7, 1777. He was then re-elected twice, serving until November 30, 1779. During his tenure, he was interested in military and naval matters. An interesting episode involved the proposed creation of a black battalion in the Rhode Island militia created from purchased slaves who had been freed. Marchant and William Ellery, his counterpart in Congress, were asked to petition Congress to raise funds to reimburse the slave masters. Ultimately, despite their best efforts, Marchant and Ellery could not convince Congress, citing the lack of funds.

Marchant was present in York, Pennsylvania, for the discussions and negotiations that resulted in the Articles of Confederation. He then signed the document on July 9, 1778. Marchant was again elected to Congress in 1780 and 1783 but did not attend. When he came up for

The stone of Henry Marchant.

election in 1784, he resigned his seat. That year, he was back in local politics as a member of the Newport Town Council. He was elected Recorder for the city and, in 1785, was elected to the state General Assembly. In 1788, Marchant was active with the committee that approved the U.S. Constitution in Rhode Island.

On April 22, 1790, during the early days of the first Washington administration, Marchant was nominated as the first federal district judge in Rhode Island. The Senate confirmed him on July 2, 1790. Early in his term, Marchant presided over *West v. Barnes* in 1791, which was the first case appealed to U.S. Supreme Court.

Marchant served as a federal judge until he died in Newport on August 30, 1796, at age 55. A local newspaper said he was "much lamented." After a well-attended funeral, he was buried in the Common Burying Ground in Newport. His tombstone reads, "The Honorable Henry Marchant. Member of the Revolutionary Congress and U.S. Judge for the District of Rhode Island. Died Aug. 30, 1796."

Rebecca Cooke Marchant died in 1819. Son William Marchant inherited the Henry Marchant Farm, a historic site located in South Kingstown, Rhode Island.

Samuel Ward
(1725 – 1776)

Colonial Governor and Continental Congressman

Common Burial Ground
Newport, Rhode Island

───── ◆ ─────

Governor • Continental Association

The son of Royal Governor of Rhode Island Richard Ward, Samuel Ward, a farmer, was also a governor and later a Continental Congressman who signed the Continental Association.

───── ◆ ─────

Ward was born on May 27, 1725, in Newport, Rhode Island, the son of Richard Ward, the Royal Governor of Rhode Island, and Mary (née Tillinghast) Ward, who was the daughter of John Tillinghast and Isabel Sayles and great-granddaughter of Roger Williams, the founder of the colony. Ward, on his father's side, was the great-grandson of John Ward, a cavalry officer in Cromwell's army, who came to America following the restoration of Charles II. Richard Ward's sister Mary Ward married Sion Arnold, a grandson of Governor Benedict Arnold II, the grandfather of the infamous traitor.

Ward was the ninth of fourteen children who grew up in a wealthy household. He was educated in the local grammar school and may have been tutored by his older brother Thomas, a Harvard graduate.

In 1745, only twenty years of age, Ward married Anna Ray, the daughter of a plantation owner on Block Island. The dowry included land on the island on which the young couple settled and began farming

Samuel Ward

and racing livestock, including Narraganset Pacers, a breed of racehorse. The couple had eleven children, including five sons and six daughters.

As a young man of thirty-one, Ward was elected a deputy from Westerly in the colonial assembly in 1756, siding on the hard money (specie) side of the ongoing paper money debate in the colony. This put him at odds with rival Stephen Hopkins of Providence, who favored paper money. The vitriol between the two was bitter, leading to a lawsuit filed by Hopkins against Ward for slander. The case was moved to Massachusetts to find an impartial court, where Ward prevailed in 1759.

Over the next ten years, Ward and Hopkins switch off in the governor's seat. In 1761, when Hopkins defeated Ward for governor, the assembly appointed Ward the chief justice of the Rhode Island Supreme Court. He held this post for one year until he was again elected governor. Ward was a proponent of the Rhode Island College, which later became

Brown University. In 1765, Ward was one of the college's founding trustees.

Despite being the Royal Governor in 1765 and 1766, Ward railed against the Stamp Act, opposing Parliament. When Rhode Island citizens protested the British tax authorities, Governor Ward did nothing to stop them and was the only colonial governor to do so. This led to the forfeiture of his position as governor, despite the act being repealed.

Hopkins won the governorship in 1767, and Ward returned home to his farm and served as a trustee of the college. As both Hopkins and Ward were no longer governors after 1768, they eventually established friendly relations.

On August 5, 1769, Ward was baptized at the age of 44 as a Seventh Day Baptist. He remained out of politics for several years.

Mrs. Anna Ward died in 1770, followed by the Boston Massacre later that year. Tensions continued to rise in Boston between the British authorities and the colonists. Following the Boston Tea Party in December 1773, the British passed the Boston Port Bill, closing the port to commerce. This led to a call for a congress to meet in Philadelphia. Both Ward and Hopkins were appointed delegates to the First Continental Congress in Philadelphia that summer, in 1774.

When the First Continental Congress met in Philadelphia, Ward kept a diary. He recapped the first day on September 5, 1774:

> Met at the New Tavern; went to Carpenter's Hall, and, liking the place, agreed to hold the Congress there; took a list of the Delegates, chose the Honorable Peyton Randolph Esq. President, and Mr. Charles Thompson Secretary; read the appointments of the Delegates; considered of the manner of each Colony's voting and rules for regulating the business; but adjourned until ten o'clock tomorrow.

Two days later, he wrote:

> Mr. [Jacob] Duché read prayers and lessons, and concluded with one of the most sublime, catholic [sic], well-adapted prayers I ever heard. Thanks for it and presented by Mr. [Thomas] Cushing [of

Massachusetts] and Mr. [Artemas] Ward [of Massachusetts]. A Committee of two from each Colony appointed to prepare a statement of those rights of the Colonists, the infringements of those rights and the means of redress. A committee to report what Acts of Parliament affect the trade of the Colonies. (45 members present.) Door keepers appointed.

Ward signed the Continental Association on October 20, 1774. He and Hopkins were then re-appointed to the Congress, attending the Continental Congress beginning in May 1775 following the battles at

Grave of Samuel Ward.

Lexington and Concord. Wrote Ward, "'Heaven save my country,' is my first, my last, and almost my only prayer." Ward devoted all of his time to the Continental Congress and served on the Committee on Secrets, and the Committee of the Whole.

In March 1776, while in Philadelphia, Ward contracted smallpox. He died on March 26, 1776, at the age of 50. Initially, Ward was buried at the First Baptist Church in Philadelphia. He was reinterred in the Common Burial Ground in Newport, Rhode Island, in 1860.

Ward's second son, Samuel Ward Jr. was a lieutenant colonel of the 1st Rhode Island Regiment in the Continental Army. Great-granddaughter Julia Ward Howe composed the "Battle Hymn of the Republic."

Westerly, Rhode Island, named its high school after Ward in 1937, but changed it to Westerly High School late in the 20th century, leaving his name on the main auditorium.

Close-up view of Samuel Ward's grave.

Sources

Books, Magazines, Journals, Files:

Appleby, Joyce. *Inheriting the Revolution: The First Generation of Americans.* Cambridge, Massachusetts: Harvard University Press, 2000.

Atkinson, Rick. *The British Are Coming: The War for America, Lexington to Princeton, 1775-1777.* New York: Henry Holt & Co. 2019.

Bordewich, Fergus M. *The First Congress: How James Madison, George Washington, and a Group of Extraordinary Men Invented the Government.* New York: Simon and Schuster Paperbacks, 2016.

Bowen, Catherine Drinker. *Miracle at Philadelphia: The Story of the Constitutional Convention May to September 1787.* Boston, Massachusetts: Little, Brown & Company, 1966.

Chambers, II, John Whiteclay. *The Oxford Companion to American Military History.* Oxford: Oxford University Press, 1999.

Commager, Henry Steele & Richard B. Morris. *The Spirit of 'Seventy-Six: The Story of the American Revolution as Told by Participants.* New York: Harper & Rowe, 1967.

Conlin, Joseph R. *The Morrow Book of Quotations in American History.* New York: William Morrow and Company, Inc., 1984.

Dann, John C. *The Revolution Remembered: Eyewitness Accounts of the War for Independence.* Chicago: University of Chicago Press, 1980.

Ellis, Joseph J. *Revolutionary Summer: The Birth of American Independence.* New York: Alfred A. Knopf, 2013.

———. *The Quartet: Orchestrating the Second American Revolution, 1783-1789.* New York: Alfred A. Knopf, 2015.

———. *His Excellency: George Washington.* New York: Alfred A. Knopf, 2004.

Flexner, James Thomas. *George Washington in the American Revolution, 1775-1783.* Boston: Little, Brown & Company, 1967.

Goodrich, Charles A. *Lives of the Signers of the Declaration of Independence.* Charlotteville, N.Y.: SamHar Press, 1976.

Grossman, Mark. *Encyclopedia of the Continental Congress.* Armenia, New York: Grey House Publishing, 2015.

Kiernan, Denise & Joseph D'Agnese. *Signing Their Lives Away: The Fame and Misfortune of the Men Who Signed the Declaration of Independence.* Philadelphia: Quirk Books, 2008.

———. *Signing Their Rights Away: The Fame and Misfortune of the Men Who Signed the United States Constitution.* Philadelphia: Quirk Books, 2011.

Klarman, Michael J. *The Framers' Coup: The Making of the United States Constitution.* New York: Oxford University Press, 2016.

Langguth, A. J. *Patriots.* New York: Simon and Schuster, 1988.

SOURCES

Lossing, Benson J. *Pictorial Field Book of the Revolution*. New York: Harper Brothers. 1851.

Maier, Pauline. *American Scripture: Making the Declaration of Independence*. New York: Alfred A. Knopf, Inc., 1997.

Middlekauff, Robert. *The Glorious Cause: The American Revolution, 1763-1789*. Oxford: Oxford University Press, 2005.

Millett, Allan R. & Peter Maslowski. *For the Common Defense: A Military History of the United States of America*. New York: The Free Press, 1984.

Moore, Charles. *The Family Life of George Washington*. New York: Houghton Mifflin, 1926.

O'Connell, Robert L. *Revolutionary: George Washington at War*. New York: Random House. 2019.

Racove, Jack N. *Revolutionaries: A New History of the Invention of America*. New York: Houghton Mifflin Harcourt, 2011.

Raphael, Ray. Founding Myths: *Stories That Hide Our Patriotic Past*. New York: MJF Books, 2004.

Rossiter, Clinton. *1787 The Grand Convention*. New York: The Macmillan Company, 1966.

Schweikart, Larry & Michael Allen. *A Patriot's History of the United States from Columbus's Great Discovery to the War on Terror*. New York: Penguin, 2004.

Sharp, Arthur G. *Not Your Father's Founders*. Avon, Massachusetts: Adams Media, 2012.

Taafee, Stephen R. *The Philadelphia Campaign, 1777-1778*. Lawrence, Kansas: University of Kansas Press, 2003.

Wood, Gordon S. *The Radicalism of the American Revolution*. New York: Vintage Books, 1993.

———. *Empire of Liberty: A History of the Early Republic, 1789-1815*. New York: Penguin Books, 2004.

———. *Revolutionary Characters: What Made the Founders Different*. New York: Penguin Books, 2006.

———. *The Americanization of Benjamin Franklin*. Oxford: Oxford University Press, 2009.

Wright, Benjamin F. *The Federalist: The Famous Papers on the Principles of American Government: Alexander Hamilton, James Madison, John Jay*. New York: Metro Books, 2002.

Video Resources:

Guelzo, Allen C. The Great Courses: *America's Founding Fathers* (Course N. 8525). Chantilly, Virginia: The Teaching Company, 2017.

Online Resources:

Archives.gov – for information on the Constitutional Convention.

ColonialHall.com – for information about the signers of the Declaration of Independence.

DSDI1776.com – for information on many Founders.

FamousAmericans.net – for information on many Founders.

FindaGrave.com – for burial information, vital statistics and obituaries.

Newspapers.com – Hundreds of newspaper articles were accessed—too numerous to mention here.

NPS.gov – for information on various park sites.

TheHistoryJunkie.com – for information on multiple Founders.

USHistory.org – for information on multiple Founders.

Wikipedia.com – for general historical information.

Index

www.ingramcontent.com/pod-product-compliance
Lightning Source LLC
Chambersburg PA
CBHW022347040426
42449CB00006B/762